"At the rising of the sun and its going down, we remember you.

At the blowing of the wind and the chill of winter, we remember you.

At the opening of the buds and in the rebirth of spring, we remember you.

At the blueness of the skies and in the warmth of summer, we remember you.

At the rustling of the leaves and in the beauty of autumn, we remember you.

At the beginning of the year and when it ends, we remember you.

As long as we live, you too will live; for you are now a part of us,

as we remember you, for now and forever, Amen."-Irish Prayer

ʃʃ

"And the stately ships go on

To their haven under the hill

But oh for the touch of a vanished hand,

And the sound of a voice that is stilled."-
Tennyson

₷

Dedication

Every book has its dedication and this one is no different. To put together a nonfiction book takes much time and effort. This book came together by quite a bit of research, walking and family participation.

I want to thank my sister Jima for willingly going on those long road trips that somehow always seemed to include a cemetery or two. She made it possible to enjoy a hobby that otherwise I probably would not get to enjoy. Over time, she has even learned to enjoy some of these places; especially Bonaventure.

I first started thinking about a book after my youngest son Tony and my daughter-in-law Krista told me about Bonaventure after one of their many trips to Savannah. Krista, who is a successful photographer, knew about my love for photographing older cemeteries and suggested that I make a point in visiting Savannah and checking it out. Never have I been so in awe of a burial ground as I was with Bonaventure. It was at this point that I wanted to record, through words and photographs, the beauty within this place. I thank them for leading me to Bonaventure's gates.

After my first visit to this historic cemetery, I quickly realized that I needed to return more than once to carefully explore the grounds. The symbolism and detail was so abundant, that it would be impossible to capture all the beauty, messages and stories that this place holds.

On one visit, I took with me three of my children, two dogs and four grandchildren; (that is a story within itself). We spent two days going up and down the paths. Not once did anyone complain about the long hours spent trying to document and record the names of persons buried there. I never heard one child asked when they could go back to the hotel or to the beach. They, themselves, were caught up with the spell that Bonaventure cast on her visitors. So I want to thank them for the gift of time that they gave to me to fulfill a dream and allow this old gal to check off another item off her bucket list.

My parents, who are now in their eighties, have been supportive with just about any ideas that I have come up with the past few years. I think they have just come to realize that I walk a different road than their other children and figured out that with me being different is all I know and find me rather amusing to see what I think up next. From cake decorating to genealogy, to coming up with the idea that I want to publish a book, they have always felt I could do it and do it well. How could I fail with support like that? So I thank my parents for believing in me.

Finally, I want to dedicate this book to those buried in Bonaventure. To the lives that once were and to their families who cared enough about them to preserve their memories in such a beautiful way, in a place that has managed for the most part, to remain pretty much as it was in the 1800's.

It is these souls that make Bonaventure different than any cemetery that I have ever had the chance to visit. It is their stories that captured my heart.

The entrance to Bonaventure Cemetery

Remember Me

Author Vera A. Turner

Within The Walls of Bonaventure Cemetery

"A people without the knowledge of their past history,
origin and culture is like a tree without roots."-Marcus Garvey

₷

The Story Tellers

I have always been intrigued with personal histories and viewed them as pieces of a very large complex puzzle. How one life, combined with another life, will create yet another story. My passion for history goes beyond my own family or what is written in the books we were given in school. The world is so much more than the few lives that wind up in our history books.

 I am a historian by nature and I enjoy reading about our past presidents, founding fathers, and the men and women who helped established my country, the United States. Without these books, they too would have passed into obscurity and the generations that came after would have known little about them.

I am what some people would call a "taphophile". A taphophile is a person who is obsessed with cemeteries. I would rather think of it more as a passion. Exploring graves is not morbid to me, but a way to make history less abstract and more real. I believe that some of us are called to be the story tellers. We have a burning desire to know about individuals who we don't even know. We become a person who seeks out others who lived years or generations before we did. We want to know about them in a personal way. We seek to make them live again so that we can know them; who they loved and who they were when they walked among the living. How did they live? How did they die? We seek for clues and we bring each piece of the puzzle to the table, where we very carefully try to put it all together until what we have is a mental photograph of who that person was. The clues give us a glimpse into their lives and then we share with others who also might feel as we do. We are genealogists who are just as interested in the neighbor who lived next door to our great-grandfathers as we are about our own families. It is this passion that gives us an appreciation and deeper respect for the past and an urgency to record the memorials that we come across.

This Thing We Call Death

We all will one day die. It is the one certainty that we have in this world. It cannot be avoided, it will happen. Death is indifferent to age, race, religion or wealth and at an appointed time, we all will experience it. We hope for a Heaven where we will have a continuation of who we are; to no longer exist is not acceptable and so we search for a way to be remembered or to be immortalized.

For many who have died, they leave those who mourn their passing, the people who remember who they were, to tell stories about them to others; but in time this will cease. Except for the few people who are written in our history books, there will come a time when no one will be left living who remembers the person that you were. How will anyone know that you once lived, that you once walked this earth, had dreams, families and a voice? Who will remember you?

Mark Twain called them the cities of the dead. We see them there as we walk or drive by but rarely give them a second thought. These cities of the dead give evidence of a time long since passed. Cemeteries have a similar unity that connects each one. The elaborate artwork of the Victorian-era tombstones of course catches attention; some are gorgeous pieces of art. But something else draws you in even more and that is the stories being told. Monument after monument, telling stories etched in stone. Many were written in prose, others in a more simplified manner, but the message was the same, Please remember me; please remember them. Wanting to believe that their lives had some sort of importance in how they lived, to prove that they were here; wanting in some way to show us who they were.

This is the purpose of this book. To give a voice to the silenced; to hear the unspoken words of the people buried within the walls of Bonaventure Cemetery and to capture their thoughts engraved on the tombstones before time, weather and erosion robs us of these thoughts. This book hopes to make them live again, to tell their stories and to feel somehow that they know and approve.

Savannah

If you have ever visited Savannah, Georgia you know that it is a city that dates back not only to the Civil War era but back to the American Revolution.   Savannah celebrates its place in history and I have never been to a city where its occupants not only know so much, but love to tell you about it. It is a place where oral history is still common and its residents take great joy in sharing what they know about Savannah's former residents. It is also considered one of the most haunted places in the United States and one of the main attractions to tourist visiting its historic city center. Though I myself have never taken one of the ghost tours, my grown children have and they are believers of the unseen occupants of downtown historic Savannah.

Located on the outskirts of Savannah is a Victorian-era cemetery called Bonaventure. Once part of a plantation, it is the final resting place of many of Savannah's former residents. It is culturally diverse with many ethnic and religious groups within the grounds.   German, Jewish, Catholic and Irish communities just to name a few of the groups of people who called Savannah their home and now are buried within the walls of Bonaventure Cemetery.

Considered by some to be haunted, Bonaventure cemetery is a favorite among ghost seekers.   Do I think it is haunted? I would have told you no if not for some of the pictures that I have taken. Many of the images and orbs visible in some of the photographs taken during my trips to the cemetery cannot be explained. Not all spirits were of the nice kind either. But that is for a different story and a different book.

Just let me say, that not everyone sleeps that peaceful and eternal rest here on the grounds of Bonaventure.

The locals like to use the cemetery for walks and visitors come to see for themselves what makes this place so special; some hoping for that "encounter".

Some of the ghost stories associated with Bonaventure include a pack of ghost dogs that are said to roam the cemetery grounds and chase people out. It is said that people have heard them breathing and barking, but I have not heard of anyone actually seeing them. Then there is the story of Little Gracie Watson, whose legend states that when visitors leave trinkets in her lap and someone takes them away, she will cry tears of blood and cry out into the night. These stories, while only just that, can't help but add to the atmosphere one imbues while walking through the cemetery. Especially, if you should visit near closing hours when it changes to an eerily quiet place and the beautiful Spanish moss that so eloquently drapes the oaks during the day takes on a more shadowy effect. I would imagine, on a stormy day when the rain pours down and the winds are bearing down on Bonaventure, it could play with someone's imagination.

The moment you pass through its gates you have stepped back into time. Large Oak trees with Spanish moss freely hanging from its limbs are everywhere. Walking through the cemetery is eerily haunting and yet beautiful at the same time. The place is absolutely lush and reminiscence of an English garden; especially when the Azaleas are in full bloom.

My favorite time to visit is early in the morning just as the gates open. The lighting for pictures is at its best and very few visitors are there yet.   As I wander through the grounds I can't help but wonder about whom these people once were. As I stop to take a picture, or to look at the carefully thought out details of some of the memorials and their symbolisms, I think about what their lives must have been like in old Savannah.

My thoughts wander to the grief their families felt as they laid their loved ones to rest and the soft intimate whisperings that they spoke over their graves. Imagining to myself the frequent and not so frequent visits of friends, relatives and sweethearts who came to just sit and visit. The loving touches to a grave from a grieving parent. These are my thoughts as I stroll within the confines of her walls.

John Muir so beautifully stated when he first visited Bonaventure and wrote in his book, *A Thousand Mile Walk,* in a chapter called *Camping among the Tombs:*

"The dead rest here it is true, but the place is alive with nature. The whole place seems like a center of life. The dead do not reign there alone. Bonaventure is called a graveyard, a town of the dead, but the few graves are powerless in such a depth of life. The rippling of living waters, the song of birds, the joyous confidence of flowers, the calm, undisturbable grandeur of the oaks, marks this place of graves as one of the Lord's most favored abodes of life. Even those spots which are disordered by art, Nature is ever at work to reclaim, and to make them look as if the foot of man had never known them."

Oscar Wilde called it "incomparable". I can't think of a more beautiful place to be buried and if you believe the ghost stories, you might be able to wander here for eternity. Not a bad thought, now is it?

Many of the earlier burials were actually transplants from Colonial Park located in the heart of Savannah and Laurel Grove cemeteries. It was considered socially acceptable in the 1800's to move family member's remains from one cemetery to another so that they could be buried near their peers and social class. Many in Savannah were moved from Colonial Park Cemetery and Laurel Grove to Bonaventure during this era.

Most impressive are the life-like monuments throughout the cemetery. You will find beautiful stained glass windows in ivy covered crypts, intrigue carvings done in the finest marble. Pink azaleas intermingle with rod iron gates. These memorials were placed on these grounds by individuals and not the cemetery itself. Loved ones bared no expense in creating lasting memorials in honor of those that passed.

This is what sets Bonaventure apart. It is a lost art that most of society doesn't bother with today. Other cemeteries are more concerned with filling the plots rather than creating a place of remembrance. The beauty and the attention to detail can be overwhelming and it takes more than one visit to Bonaventure to take it all in.

With all the beauty that encompasses Bonaventure, one common thread jumps out and that common thread is that these are people that once lived; they mattered to someone. Their families, through these monuments, are asking you to remember them. If you listen, you can hear their stories being repeated in the warm southern breeze. There are so many stories to be heard and told. This book captures only a few of them but in sharing them, perhaps they will encourage you to visit and listen for yourself.

A Little History on Bonaventure

Bonaventure Cemetery is full of history and it is truly a visual history lesson of old Savannah in the late 1700 and 1800's. Step through her gates and her dead start talking to you in ways you never thought possible. The haunting beauty of the Spanish moss as it drapes from the limbs of the live oaks, draws you further into her grounds to explore. The excitement, reverence and respect for these former lives that one discovers just beyond the next path is undeniable. Though their eyes have closed, it is as if they see you wander through the maze of paths and they want you to know that it is alright to visit; to pause and to take a moment to *see* them.

Azaleas, roses, magnolias, and dogwoods almost hypnotize the senses and you can't help but to get caught up in the romantic feel of the place. Little wonder past generations felt differently about cemeteries than their descendants. Savannah's cemeteries were built into the park system and it wasn't uncommon to find families visiting their friends and families along with a picnic lunch and perhaps a drink or two, enjoying the lush greenery that Bonaventure Cemetery is known for.

"Where there is sorrow there is holy
ground."
-Wilde
℔

Colonial Garden is a section where many of Savannah's founding Fathers can be found and the earlier settlers.

Mullryne and Tattnall

When I first started researching the historical background on Bonaventure, it was a bit confusing because of the names of the owners. To save you this frustration, I will tell you now that there are three different Josiah Tattnall's. Knowing this will make the following information easier to follow and to understand.

Bonaventure Plantation was first settled by John Mullryne in 1760 after being given a land grant for the purpose of planting. He named it after a French word "Buena Ventura" which translated means "good fortune". Despite the name's meaning the plantation had its share of troubles. During the French invasion, when France was trying to capture Savannah from the British, it was occupied by the French armies and used as a hospital and most likely many French soldiers are buried on Bonaventure's grounds. The original plantation burned in 1771. Folk lore states that the Tattnall's were having a dinner party when the fire broke out. Not wanting to be poor hosts, they had the dinner moved outside and continued the event while the fire burned. Some visitors to Bonaventure have claimed to hear people laughing and glasses breaking to this day where the home once stood. It was replaced with a red brick mansion and it was one of Savannah's finest plantations.

When John Mullryne's youngest daughter Mary, married Josiah Tattnall, it is said that he marked the event with the planting of live oak trees along the avenue leading to the plantation in such a way that they formed a monogram combining the initials of both families M&T. Mary and Josiah had two children that were born at Bonaventure; John Mullryne Tattnall born 1763 and Josiah Tattnall Jr. born in 1765.

Both Mullryne and Tattnall had over 9,000 acres between them including the 600 acres three miles outside of Savannah near St. Augustine Creek and overlooking the Wilmington River that comprised Bonaventure Plantation.

At the time, the United States was still under England's rule with the Revolutionary War underway. Many were loyal to King George III (Tories) and publically announced their loyalty to England. Because of this loyalty they were banished from the state of Georgia. John Mullryne and Josiah Tattnall were two such loyalists. Although they would have been ordered to leave the state, I cannot find documents supporting that they ever left Georgia.

Their land was seized by the government and sold at auction. Josiah died at the early age of thirty-six. His wife,

Mary, died shortly thereafter, leaving their children orphaned. Distant relatives, perhaps their grandparents, brought the children back to London, England where they were raised.

Their son Josiah Tattnall Jr., who was 10 at the time of his parent's death, had recalled fond memories of growing up on the plantation and at sixteen, moved back to Savannah. It should be mentioned that though his parents were loyal to England they refused to take up arms against their beloved state of Georgia. Their plantation was confiscated by the British, sold at auction and it was purchased by John Habersham. Records show that after the war, because of the Tattnall's loyalty to Georgia and in appreciation, John Habersham sold the property back to Josiah Jr. in 1788.

As an adult, Josiah joined the United States Navy and eventually became a commodore. Commodore Josiah Tattnall Jr. married Harriette Fenwick. They had nine children; four were buried on the Plantation's grounds. Harriet died in 1873 and was the first adult to be buried in Bonaventure. She was buried next to her four children. Josiah Tattnall died two years later in 1875 in Nassau and was brought home to be buried next to his family. At this time, it was a small private family burial cemetery within the plantation. In an ironic twist, Commander Tattnall's beloved Bonaventure was confiscated yet again by the federal government during the Civil War when he refused to remain in the service of the United States Navy and take up arms against Georgia. The property was eventually returned to their ownership.

The last Tattnall, Josiah Tattnall III and his brother Edward Fenwick Tattnall never lived at Bonaventure and in 1846, sold their inheritance to Captain Peter Wiltberger, who was the owner of the Pulaski House in Savannah. The plantation was sold with the stipulation that he maintained the burial plots even though it was not included in the sale. This was a promise that he kept and was later buried there himself.

Peter Wiltberger's son created a company and set aside 70 acres for a private cemetery which was later called Evergreen Cemetery Company. He sold the cemetery in 1907 to the city of Savannah. The city restored the named of Bonaventure Cemetery.

The Tattnall family lot is in section E in Bonaventure in what is called the Colonial Garden. Many of Savannah's founding families can be found in this section. What started out as a small family cemetery evolved into 160 acres and at this time is still an active cemetery and has a few burial plots available for sell.

Commodore Josiah Tattnall. U.S. & C.S.
Born near this spot Nov. 9th 1795 Died June 14th 1875

The Tattnall family plot

"Harriette Fenwick Wife of Commodore Josiah Tattnall

"They shall grow not old, as we that are left grow old:
Age shall not weary them, nor the years condemn.
At the going down of the sun and in the morning,
We will remember them."-Laurence Bonyon

ß

Gracie Watson
1883-1889
Plot: Section E Lot 98

LITTLE GRACIE
LITTLE GRACIE WATSON WAS BORN
ONLY CHILD OF HER PARENTS HER FATHER
MANAGER OF THE PULASKI HOUSE, ONE OF
SAVANNAH'S LEADING HOTELS, WHERE THE
BEAUTIFUL AND CHARMING LITTLE GIRL WAS A
FAVORITE WITH THE GUESTS. TWO DAYS BEFORE
EASTER, IN APRIL 1889, GRACIE DIED OF
PNEUMONIA AT THE AGE OF SIX. IN 1890, WHEN
THE RISING SCULPTOR JOHN WALZ MOVED TO
SAVANNAH, HE CARVED FROM A PHOTOGRAPH
THIS LIFE-SIZED, DELICATELY DETAILED MARBLE
STATUE, WHICH FOR ALMOST A CENTURY HAS
CAPTURED THE INTEREST OF ALL PASSERSBY.

There are many children buried here at Bonaventure, some were loss to the yellow fever epidemic that swept Savannah during the 1800's, others to pneumonia, childhood illness and other causes. I cannot think of anything harder to bear than the death of one's child. The emptiness, silence and heartbreak from such a loss can be inconsolable; especially if they were your only child. Can you imagine the grief?

Gracie is probably one of Bonaventure's more famous residents. Many believe that she haunts her burial site and that of her former home, The Pulaski House, where her father was resident manager. She was the only child of Wales J. and Frances M. Watson. The Watsons came from Vermont where Wales had worked as a hotel supervisor.

The 1880 census shows that he & Frances, both twenty four at the time, were living with his sister and her husband in Vermont. Sometime after 1880, He and his wife accepted the resident manager position to the Pulaski House, a leading hotel in Savannah at the time. Being Northerners moving into a Southern community in the 1800's, his wife, Frances probably would have found it hard to fit in with Savannah's elite. When researching information about Frances, it has been written that she was a clever woman and learned to use the hotel to her advantage. Related stories say that Frances held numerous parties where she invited the socialites of Savannah and soon she was accepted within the group. Gracie was at all these affairs and stories say that she was a favorite during these events; especially by those that were frequent hotel guests; She was in a way, Savannah's little hostess and was known by many as the sweetheart of Savannah.

The Pulaski House was the only home that Gracie ever knew in her short life and she would play throughout the hotel; probably to the amusement of the hotel guests. When she took ill with pneumonia at the age of six and died two days before Easter, I can imagine that the entire city of Savannah felt the loss and grieved with her parents.

Wales and Frances Watson laid their only daughter to rest at Bonaventure Cemetery. One can only envision the heavy hearts and tears that fell as they brought their little girl through the gates of the cemetery that day.

At first, she had a smaller headstone. Later her father commissioned John Walz, a sculptor, who had done other work for Savannah, to create a memorial for his beloved daughter. The sculpture was created from a photograph given to Walz by her father. It has been said that when Wales gave the family photograph of Gracie to John Walz he could not speak because of his grief.

The amazing piece of art that John Walz created marks Gracie Watson's plot in Bonaventure now. Her burial site has become so popular by tourist that an iron fence now surrounds her grave to protect it from vandalism and those just wanting to touch it. Stories say that visitors can hear her cry and that sometimes tears appear on the statue itself. Others say they can hear a child laughing at her former home which is now one of the dorms at Savannah College of Arts & Design. These are all stories and certainly add to the haunted aspect of Savannah's history.

It has been said that Gracie's father sunk into a deep depression and that the Watson's left Savannah for Washington DC. Public records show otherwise.

The Watson's did leave the Pulaski House. With a Mr. Powers, Wales became a co-proprietor of the Desoto House in Savannah up to July 1904. If the Watsons left Savannah, it was at a later time. I am not quite sure when the statue was commissioned, but it could have been done before they left the city for good in remembrance of a daughter that they were sadly leaving behind.

 Both Wales & Frances died in New York. Wales died October 4, 1919 at the age of 63 and his wife died December 26, 1913 at the age of 56. Her death certificate stated she had ulcerations on the breast so she could possibly have died from breast cancer. The later census does not show them having any other children. They both are buried in Menands, New York, Albany Rural Cemetery.

**The cut tree stump represents a life cut
Short and the ivy symbolizes memory**

Gracie Watson's memorial has become so popular
that an iron fence was built around her gravesite to
protect the statue from further damage. Gracie's nose
was chipped by boys throwing rocks. She remains
one of the most photographed memorials within
Bonaventure Cemetery.

It is said that the first time Mr. Watson saw
The statue
He exclaimed "that is Gracie!"

You can see in the photograph the damage to Gracie's nose by children throwing rocks and why the fence was built around her to prevent further damage to her memorial

"Then is it sin to rush into the house of death, Ere death dare come to us?"- Shakespeare

§§

Corinne Elliot Lawton

1844- Jan24, 1877

"Allured to Brighter Worlds and
Led the Way"

Plot: Section H Lot 168

Losing a child through illness or accident is hard enough, but to know that you somehow had a part in that death would be even harder. When your child takes their own life, your life becomes full of what ifs... If only I said this or had I done that differently, then perhaps she would still be here. "Anyone who has been close to someone that has taken their life knows, there is no other pain like that felt after the incident."(Peter Greene)

Right here in Bonaventure is yet another story similar to Romeo & Juliet. A story as old as time itself; the story of forbidden love and the despair that lost love brought to one family. Can it get any more heartbreaking? This is the story of Corinne Lawton, another popular gravesite in Bonaventure.

Corinne was the first born daughter of Alexander Robert Lawton. His importance in Savannah's history is well documented. A Brigadier General in the Confederate Army, he also was a president of the Augusta Savannah Railroad, a politician, president of the American Bar Association and well known in the arts and theater community in Savannah.

According to stories from local folklore, Corrine was in love with someone below her station. Her father would not allow the relationship and took it upon himself to find her a more suitable match and she was to be married. There are so many stories about this event. It has been said that Corrine was inconsolable and heartbroken. The story relates that weeks before her death, she stopped eating and refused visitors. Her depression became worse with each passing day. The day before she was to be married she went out to Bonaventure, presumably by horse and carriage. Because Bonaventure is located on the outskirts of historical Savannah, it would have been a long drive in those days by horse. She must have left quite early to make it there without someone stopping her. It is there she threw herself off the bluff of the Wilmington River and drowned the night before her wedding.

It has been reported that she died of cystic fibrous but I do not know if that account is accurate. Another account of her death is that she was hot with fever and threw herself off the bluff. Personal letters of her father have him writing to a business correspondence about another yellow fever outbreak a few months before her death, but he had taken his family out of Savannah to avoid the outbreak.

The story that you will hear on tours is the one that I have told you and it does add to the romantic despair of young love and to Bonaventure's allure. Her obituary in the Savannah News made no mention of how she died. Dated Jan. 25, 1877 it simply stated "Lawton- the friends and acquaintances of General & Mrs. A.R. Lawton are invited to attend the funeral of their eldest daughter, Corinne, this morning at 11 o'clock from their residence 135 Perry Street."

During this time period of religious history in regards with suicide, the soul was not permitted in Heaven. I imagine that if the cause of her death was a suicide, then it would have been kept as quiet as possible.

I do not believe that her father was being mean and spiteful but in his own way felt that he was protecting his daughter. Historically at this time, many women did not work and had no means to support themselves. A good marriage is what assured them of a financially solid life that someone like Corrine, because of her father's wealth, had been accustomed to her entire life. I believe that he only wanted his daughter to have those things she would need and want. He was close to his daughter and probably had he known the outcome, he would have arranged things so that his daughter could marry the person she truly loved. But he didn't know, he didn't change things and that is what is so sad about Corrine's passing. Love was both her blessing and curse.

In her life, Corinne and her father were well acquainted with the arts and attended many performances together. He built a performing arts hall in his daughter's memory where the St. Paul Greek Orthodox Church now stands on the corner of Anderson & Bull Street.

Corinne was initially buried at Laurel Grove Cemetery. Her father died while in Clifton Springs New York in 1896 from heart failure. He also was originally buried in Laurel Grove. Both remains were removed to Bonaventure on April 26, 1898.

The Lawton family burial lot is one of the most beautiful in Bonaventure. Corrine's memorial is breathtaking. Her family spared no expense in their daughter's memory. The family commissioned the sculptor Benedetto Civiletti from Palermo Sicily to create a statue in memory of their daughter. Corrine is sitting at the foot of a cross, clothed in a robe with a bare left shoulder. Her left hand is palm up and a wreath lies at her feet as if it had been dropped from her hand. It is intricately detailed and said to be of her likeness.

I find it interesting that she has her back to other family members and her statue sits in the left corner of the lot. Sculptor Professor R. Romandlit of Florence Italy created another large arched monument with a larger than life-size statue of Christ that honors General Lawton's memory in 1898. The sculpture has a statue of Christ standing next to the arch which represents the gateway to Heaven. Again, what impresses me is how Corinne's does not face the arch. The way her memorial is sitting she faces away from the family plot.

Understanding the religion beliefs of the Victorian-era, the taking of one's own life would exclude that person from entering Heaven. Perhaps that is why she sits at the foot of the cross with an opened hand with what appears to be a dropped wreath. The cross perhaps symbolizing Christ's mercy. She is also facing east. Christ, it is said, will appear from the East when he returns. Could she be waiting for His return to plead for mercy and the reason the wreath is not in her hand? (The wreath symbolizes eternity) These are only guesses. The people that could answer those questions have also since passed away. The only things that remain are the stories. For me, it is the personal hell that her parents lived here on Earth after losing someone who was loved beyond measure. The pain that they must have felt, the constant wondering if only.........

It is near here by the bluff that it is said Corrine Drowned herself rather than marry someone she Did not love.

The statue is said to be of Corrine's likeness

It looks as if she dropped the wreath;
Because the wreath symbolizes eternity,
I can't help but wonder if it may be that she
Let eternity fall from her hands.

Sitting at the foot of the cross, her right hand is set over the left, palm facing up. I love the bare shoulder and it is seen on many memorials.

With her back to her father's grave, Christ looks towards
Corrine's burial plot as if to be beckoning with his hand to
The "Gate to Heaven" It is inscribed with the words
"Heirs together of the Grace of Life"

She sits with her back to the rest of the family.
I found this to be interesting and can't help
But wonder if it was for Biblical reasons.

The artist was able to rest her foot in such a way that it
Allowed her gown to flow off the steps

Corrine's father Alexander Robert Lawton's
memorial. It is one of Bonaventure's most beautiful.

I shot this photo from such an angle as to see the road continue after entering the archway. I believe life continues after our journey here.

Marie M. Barclay Taliaferro
July 25 1858 – February 15 1893
Plot: Section E Lot 96

Sometimes when looking for a story we find something entirely different than what was intended. Such is the story of Marie Taliaferro.

The final resting place of this woman sits next to that of Gracie Watson. It was while visiting Gracie's burial site that the intrigue for me began. I wanted to know her story.

A life-size angel watches over her mortal remains and the details of the angel are exquisite. Though time has brought with it a broken wing and fingers, she is still quite beautiful. The Taliaferro memorial was thoughtfully created; an angel with an extended hand placing a palm leaf over a cross which represents the victory over death. It is one of the most beautiful memorials I have seen in Bonaventure. She not quite thirty-five at the time of her death and I wanted to learn more about her.

To know this woman, I had to step back two generations to that of her maternal grandparents James and Mary Magdalene Marshall.

Mary Magdalene Marshall born around 1783 and was the only daughter of Gabriel and Mary Schick Leaver. Originally from England, he was a prosperous and well known cabinet maker in the southern coastal town in Savannah. Gabriel and Mary's parents were most likely part of the group of original settlers that came to Savannah with Oglethorpe.

Although Mary's father died at an early age of 38, he had acquired numerous properties and left his wife and daughter a comfortable life. She acquired this inheritance when her mother died. Mary Marshall became one of Savannah's wealthiest women through her own smart business dealings. One such business venture was a hotel called The Marshall House. Mary felt that the city could use another hotel to accommodate its ever growing number of visitors. During the civil war it was occupied by the union army and used as a hospital. Considered to be haunted, it had been renovated through the years and has become a very popular tourist attraction in Savannah's historic district. So many tourists have reported having paranormal encounters while staying there, that it is said the hotel keeps a journal of them. The hotel has also been showcased in television programs documenting haunted places in the United States.

Through newspaper clippings we know that Mary Magdalene Leaver married James Marshall of St. Augustine Florida at the age of 16 October 30, 1800. They had by all accounts, a very long and happy marriage that lasted 45 years before James died at the age of 65.

Both were involved with the volunteer guard during the Civil War, opening their home to wounded soldiers. Because of the devotion, James Marshall was given a full escort by the volunteer corps when he died as a way of honoring him and his contributions to the city.

Through documents and clippings, it is clear that they were heavily involved in raising money and working for such causes as the widows with dependent children and the Savannah asylum for women. During this time, the Marshalls adopted an infant girl, whom they called

Margaret. James was already sixty years old and Mary fifty-six. Why they waited so long and decided to adopt at such a late age is a mystery.

Family papers show that they adopted Margaret in 1841 and that she was baptized that same year. The papers also lead us to believe that their new daughter was adopted from a local Irish family and that she was one of ten children. The name of the family has been deleted from the records at the request of the Marshall family. This document can be found at the Georgia Historical society.

James died 5 years later and so Mary Marshall raised their new daughter alone.

When their daughter Margaret was barely in her teens, she met and married another prominent Savannah resident by the name of Anthony Adalbert Ethelston Waldburg Barclay. He was the son of a British consul in New York and was well known in diplomatic circles. The Savannah News posted the wedding announcement "married by Rt. Rev. Elliot, DDA Adalbert E.W. Barclay Esq. youngest son of Her Majesty's consul at New York to Miss Margaret Marshall of Savannah GA".

It should have been an exciting time for Margaret who was 14 or 15 at the time of her marriage. He was twenty-one. Instead it was the opposite. In their brief marriage they had three children; two died in infancy. They had only child, their daughter Mary (Marie), who survived.

Margaret filed for divorced in 1859 at the age of eighteen charging Adlabert with intoxication, physical abuse and adultery. I can't help think that she was able to file for divorce because of her Grandmother's standing in the community. Divorce was not that common in the mid-1800s and it would have been the subject of much gossip. Margaret, herself, died young at the age of twenty-five.

Mary Marshall's granddaughter's relationship with her father had been completely severed with the divorce so once again, at the age of eighty; Mary took over raising her granddaughter after Margaret's death. With her wealth, she most likely had the help of tutors and governesses to help raise Mary (Marie).   If Mary was anything like her grandmother then she grew an exceptional woman.

When Mary Marshall died at the age of ninety-three, Mary (Marie) Barclay became the sole heir to the Marshall estate. She met and married a school teacher by the name of Charles Champe Taliaferro in 1891. He served in the Confederate Army and after the war he became a school teacher. Records show that a John Taliaferro was the principal at a boy's academy and I can't help but wonder if this was an Uncle or brother who offered him a position if he came to Savannah. He was in Savannah several years before he married Mary. Charles also came from a prominent family from Mt. Sharon, Virginia. Her inheritance enabled them to live a very comfortable life. Mary died in 1893 at the age of thirty- four, leaving behind three children; Frances Armistead, Charles Champe Jr. and Albert Barclay Taliaferro. Her husband took their children and moved back to Mt. Sharon, Virginia after his wife's death. You can tell what he felt for his wife by this incredible memorial that he had placed before he and his children left. As with many of the memorials I encountered, my thoughts wandered back into time when a young father brought his three young children to bury their mother.

Her daughter, Frances, became the eventual sole heir to the remaining Marshall Estate. All of the properties were sold in time and none of the descendants hold any ownership of the properties nor do any family members remain in Savannah.

I am so glad that I came across her burial site and took the time to learn her story. Other than the elaborate memorial, there is nothing that would tell someone that she was the granddaughter of one of Savannah's prominent and wealthiest citizens.

Marie Taliaferro's mother and grandparents are buried in Laurel Grove Cemetery and only Mary (Marie) is buried in Bonaventure.

The detail of this memorial is incredible and
Carefully thought out in both design and symbolism,
(Columns that are short; palm leaf, cross, crowns)
Pictures cannot capture all of its beauty.
This is certainly one that you must see in person and my favorite
to photograph.

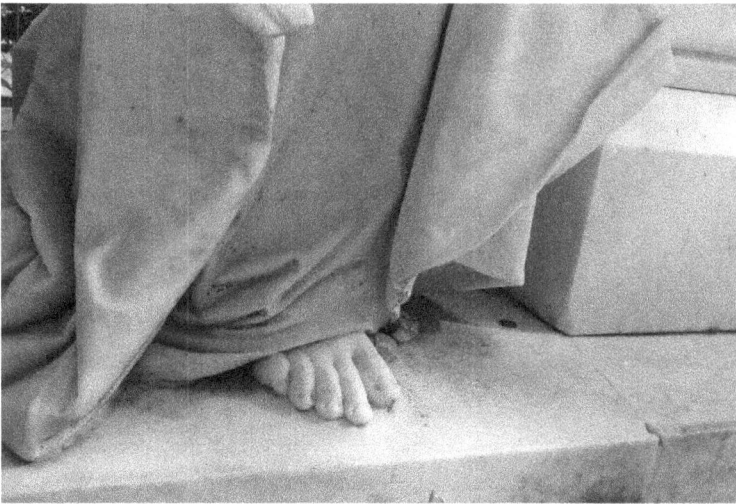

Time has caused damage to the fingers of this angel
And to one of her wings; I sometimes refer to her
As my broken angel

"Step softly, a dream lies here."-author unknown

"I saw an angel in the marble and carved until I set it free." - Michangleo."

⨎

John Walz
1844-1922
Plot: Section A Lot # 331

How is it that the man who gave so much beauty to Savannah and its occupants is remembered by a simple wooden cross? Especially in a place as beautiful as Bonaventure that has hundreds of gorgeous and elaborate memorials? I find it amazing that the burial site of John Walz, the German born sculptor who created many of Bonaventure's memorials, does not have one of his own.

Just who is John Walz? You may not recognize the name but you probably would recognize some of his works. He created the baptismal font for the Episcopal Church at Abercorn and 34th street and the beautifully detailed memorial to Gracie Watson was also one of his creations. There are over seventy statues in Bonaventure alone that were carved by John Walz. So why does a man who gave so much of himself left with just a piece of wood to remind us where he is buried?

Walz moved to Philadelphia from Germany to live with his sister after the death of his parents when he was about 14. He later moved back to Europe to study art and sculpture and eventually had a career there. His employer was commissioned by Savannah for large statues for the Telfair Art Museum. Walz helped work on the statues and then accompanied them to Georgia. He fell in love with the city and eventually moved to Savannah at the request of his brother Charles. At one time he had two studios opened to accommodate his work requests.

He married late in life. At the age of 63 he married Sara Bell Gilmore. For whatever reason, Sara destroyed his drawings and notes after his death. For all the beautiful memorials that he created for others, his wife did not honor her husband with one of his own. Sara is buried between first husband Charles Gilmore and an unmarked grave, which I am only guessing is that of her second husband John Walz. Both she and her first husband have headstones. Why, she did not make sure he had his own memorial is a mystery to me. Especially when during his lifetime it was a way to honor and immortalize the deceased. We may never know why she did the things she did. Was it because of financial reasons? Perhaps, it was his wish that his drawings and notes be destroyed at his death, and perhaps it was also his wish to not have a stone created for him. I think of this when I start to Judge Sara. We do not know what her personal relationship with her husband was nor do we know what was spoken between the two of them in regards to his own death and burial wishes. Knowing this, I still find it sad that the man who gave so much to Savannah was not given the honor that he so richly deserved. The Bonaventure historical society must have felt the same way as a memorial lawn was created in his memory and was dedicated in April 2012 and plans are being made to have his own memorial created.

John Walz (source unknown on this photo)

**The garden was dedicated in April, 2010
To John Walz and erected by the Bonaventure
Historical Society 2012.**

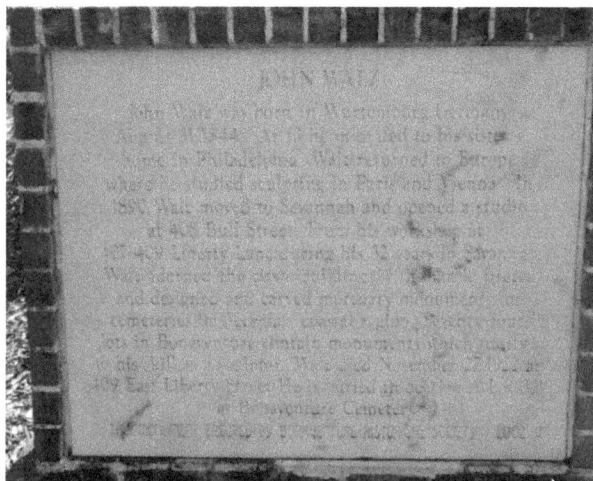

The Plaque in recognition of John Walz's contribution
 To the city of Savannah and her residents sits in the garden
Area that honors Mr. Walz.
Reads: "John Walz was born in Wurttemberg, Germany
August 31, 1844. At 13 he migrated to his sister's
 Home in Philadelphia. Walz returned to Europe
Where he studied sculpting in Paris and Vienna. In 1890,
Walz moved to Savannah and opened a studio at
 408 Bull Street.
 From his workshop at 407-409 Liberty Lane
 During his 32 years in Savannah Walz adorned
The city's buildings with marbles friezes and designed
 And carved mortuary monuments for cemeteries in
 Georgia's coastal region. Seventy four lots in
 Bonaventure contain monuments which testify to his
 Skill as a sculptor. Walz died November 27, 1922 at
 409 East Liberty Street.
 He is buried in Section A Lot 331 at Bonaventure Cemetery.

Works of John Walz

Whenever I visit Bonaventure Cemetery I look for memorials carved by John Walz I love his attention to detail and seeing the difference between his earlier and later carvings

Barbara Ruckert lies in the plot left to J.A. Schafer's. The angel is holding a palm leaf and crown representing victory over death and immortality

I am always looking for his name on the memorials.
Most master sculptors will sign their designs.

Andre Louis son of T. and A. Desbouillons
September 1, 1906- April 14, 1908
Such is the Kingdom of Heaven

There are over 70 memorials sculpted by John Walz
In Bonaventure. I have only found 12 so far.
I consider finding them my own personal treasure hunt
Whenever I visit.

John Walz's attention to detail shows why he is
A master sculptor; Notice all the symbols that he put
Into the design:
Winged hourglass (time flies) Palm leaf (resurrection),
Burial cloth (mourning)

Sculpture by John Walz. The intricate details
Can be seen close up in the photo above. It is the
Memorial of JA Shafer and can be found
In Section "A" plot 185. The tree stump is
Symbolic of a life cut short. The other symbols
Found on this piece alone include the winged
Hourglass, palm leave, ivy
And mourning cloth.

The burial plot of Charles Gilmore and Sarah Gilmore Walz
Along with the unmarked grave of John Walz.
Charles was Sarah's first husband.

Harry Hervey
1900-1951
Plot: Section T Lot:

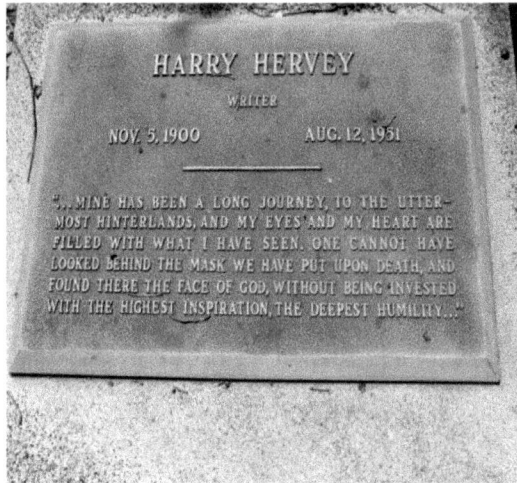

What a life! You can't help but stand at this man's gravesite and imagine all the places he has been and not be a little envious of all of his experiences and adventures that this one life experienced.

Named after his deceased father, Author and playwright Harry Hervey, was born in Beaumont, Texas and lived quite a number of years in Savannah at the Desoto Hotel where his mother, Jane Louise Davis, was the resident manager of housekeeping from around 1923 up to 1957. This is the same hotel that Gracie Watson's father was co-proprietor of when they left the Pulaski House after Gracie's death.

Hervey loved writing since he was about eight and is said to have sold his first work at the age of sixteen. He wrote such novels as *The Damned Don't Cry*, which was set in Savannah and was published in 1939. The book was very provocative in its time. He is also given writing credits for at least 12 Hollywood productions including *Shanghai Express* which starred Marlene Dietrich and *Road to Singapore* with Bob Hope and Bing Crosby. His work also included writing for stage productions.

Harry never married but he did have a lifelong companion in a man named Alonzo Carleton Hildreth. It was while working in New York, that he met Alonzo, a working actor at the time. While Carleton acted in his younger years, he seems to have worked very little during the depression and by personal papers he obviously devoted his life to Harry. Harry Hervey made no secret in the fact that he was gay nor did it seem to hurt his career any; at least in Hollywood.

His extensive travels gave Harry an endless supply of writing ideas, which is probably why he was able to transform his travels into novels that attracted Hollywood. His travels reflected in his writings. His visit through India became the novel *Caravans by Night*; travels to Singapore became *The Road to Singapore*. Many more titles and stories follow in the same way. You can understand why his novels were so successful because the attention to detail.

He had been to these countries, experienced the cultures and people personally. Hervey was able to capture in his writings the experiences so vividly that he was able to create that perfect story.

Passport applications and other travel ledgers document his travels to France, Palestine, Java, Singapore, British India, Egypt, Italy and England. His passport always stating the reason for his travels was pleasure. He would be gone almost a year with some of his trips. The passenger lists on the ports of departure almost always included Hildreth.

The Georgia Historical Society has done a wonderful job in their collection of Savannah's history and it is a treasure trove waiting to be uncovered if you take the time to read through all the information that has been collected. They have a collection of Harry's and Hildreth's personal letters to each other. By reading them, it allows a rare glance into the life of a gay couple in Savannah in the early and mid-1900.

Letters written between Harry and Carleton while Harry was working in Hollywood showed that they indeed were a couple and that relationship was widely known. They would mention visiting each other's families even when they were apart. The letters spoke about weight, money issues, fidelity, and other subjects that any couple would write in letters to their significant other while one was away. Harry took great pains to reassure Carleton that nothing but business was going on when he worked around soldiers.

Harry Hervey died of throat cancer in 1951 at the age of fifty one. In an open letter that was printed in The Savannah News shortly before his death in 1951 he wrote, "Whether I live or die-I and thousands of others-depend morally upon you, upon your enlightment and your generosity." He was appealing for funds to help a local cancer fund drive while lying in his death bed." He later succumbed to cancer. His memorial was held August 14, 1951 at Sipple's Mortuary in Savannah.

He left his personal papers to his partner which Carleton kept. It has been said that the papers were loss for a while after Hildreth died but resurfaced again after the republication of Hervey's novel. Carleton is not buried near his life partner as I would have thought he would be. He died in Savannah, Georgia but I do not know where he is buried. Harry Hervey is buried next to his Mother. I would like to believe that being buried in Bonaventure was of his choosing. It is a suitable resting place for such a writer as he was. He rests in good company along with other poets, writers and actors that are also buried in Bonaventure.

Midnight in the Garden of Good & Evil

The Bird Girl

Bonaventure became well known after John Berendant's novel and the subsequent movie Midnight in the Garden of Good And Evil came out in 1994 and the cemetery has never been the same since. To say that the movie had a huge impact on both Savannah and Bonaventure cemetery would be putting it mildly. Believing that the statue is still in Bonaventure Cemetery, tourists come from around the world to get a glimpse of the famed statue that was used as the cover for the book.

The title refers to the voodoo belief that at midnight there is a window to use both good and evil magic and the garden refers to in this instance to Bonaventure Cemetery.

The statue was created in Lake Forest, Illinois around 1936 by a renowned sculptor by the name of Sylvia Shaw Judson. She created four of these statues. One was purchased by the Trosdal family, who renamed the piece Wendy and placed it at the family plot in Bonaventure. It set there undisturbed for years until after the book came out. It was removed from Bonaventure in 1993.

Random House hired a local photographer from the Savannah area to create a cover for the Book Midnight in the Garden of Good and Evil. The author John Berendt suggested looking within the walls of Bonaventure Cemetery. At the end of his second day of searching, he came across a statue of a young girl which quickly became known as "The Bird Girl". He had to shoot rather quickly as it was getting dark and is said to have spent hours editing the photo in his studio.

The Trosdal family decided to remove the statue because of all the traffic to their family plot and lent it to the Telfair museum in Savannah. Telfair museum is still its current home. I wish that the family would have built a fence instead so that visitors could enjoy the statue the way it was intended but their concern is understandable.

This should be a reminder to the visitors that Bonaventure is sacred grounds and some do not want others wandering through their lots. Bonaventure is unusual because of its increased popularity since the release of the book and movie. Savannah wants its visitors to enjoy Bonaventure yet respect its grounds at the same time. The heavy traffic is starting to show shifting of the memorials due to the vibrations of cars and tour buses driving through and I wonder how long it will be before driving tours will be disallowed. I wonder if John Berendant, John Williams, his family and the city of Savannah could ever imagine the impact this book, subsquent movie and especially the bird girl statue have had since its release. To me, it has been like a two-edged sword in that it put both Savannah and Bonaventure Cemetery at the top of vacation spots. And with that new found popularity came the problem of showcasing them both and maintaining the balance with nature and preservation.

Jim Williams

The subject of John Berendt's book was Jim Williams. He was a well-respected antique dealer and restorer of historical homes in Savannah. Jim Williams was accused of murdering who some say was a local prostitute and part time employee of his by the name of Danny Hansford, on May 2, 1981 in his home. Jim said that it was self-defense while others say it was a lover's quarrel. The only one that truly knows is the two men involved and since both of them are now deceased one can only assume. It is a non-fictional book that reads like a novel which is what probably made it so popular.

Dorothy Kingery, Jim Williams's sister, has stated that the book takes many liberties and has a lot more fiction in it. She has written a book about her brother that clarifies different aspects about Jim and his trial. I should say trails, as he was tried 4 different times. The first trial he was convicted but appealed. The second trial he was convicted again and sentenced to life in prison but the judge overturned it and granted a third trial because someone had lied on the stand. The third trial ended with a hung jury and a subsequent mistrial. A fourth trial was allowed to be moved to an area outside of Savannah to Augusta. It was here that he was finally acquitted of the murder. It has been said that Jim Williams was the first person ever to be tried four times for murder in the state of Georgia.

Jim William's sister, Dorothy, stated that her brother allowed Jim Berendt, whom he had only met once while he was still in prison, to write the story to clear his name. Jim never got to see the finished book. He died four years before the book was released and six months after he was released from prison. He died from a major heart attack in 1990 in the same room where he shot Hansford. You can't help but believe that having to go on trial four different times didn't lead up to his death. That kind of stress can kill anyone.

Many people think that because of Bonaventure Cemetery's part in the book and movie that Jim Williams is buried there but that is not true. He was laid to rest next to his mother Blanche Brooks Williams in Gordon, Georgia.

The Live Oak Trees of Bonaventure

A Big part of Bonaventure's appeal is its beautiful Oak trees that have Spanish moss draping from her limbs. A book about this cemetery would not be complete without including information about the trees. I could not give better information than what the city of Savannah's department of Cemetery wrote, so I have quoted them in the description.

"Bonaventure has long been known for the massive live oak trees with arched limbs covered in Spanish moss overhanging her roadways. Historical documentation has proved that many of the live oak trees in Bonaventure today are nearly 250 years old. When Colonel John Mullryne selected this site for his family's residence in 1764, he directed the establishment of live oak trees every fifteen feet along both sides of the main corridors of the estate.

These trees were well established before the American Revolution.

Live oak has a naturally spiraling wood grain that allows the tough wood to bend rather than break, making the tree the most hurricane-resistant tree in North America. The most ferocious storm ever to strike Savannah was the Hurricane of 1804 at the beginning of a century and the second worst was the Great Sea Islands Hurricane at the end of the same century (1893). Other major hurricanes struck in 1824, 1854 and 1884, with intermittent hurricanes of less force and tropical storms too numerous to mention. These were the glory days of the hurricane-resistant live oaks at Bonaventure which survived and even thrived during repeated poundings by gale force winds.

The trees have been slowly declining since the Great Sea Islands Hurricane of 1893; however, there are two and a half centuries of surveys, photographs, reports, and folklore that have documented their life story. In 2004, the live oaks of Bonaventure Cemetery were registered on the Georgia Landmark and Historic Tree Register." (City of Savannah Dept. of Cemetery)."

"The most conspicuous glory of Bonaventure is its noble avenue of live-oaks. They are the most magnificent planted trees I have ever seen, about fifty feet high and perhaps three or four feet in diameter, with broad spreading leafy heads. The main branches reach out horizontally until they come together over the driveway, embowering it throughout its entire length, while each branch is adorned like a garden with ferns, flowers, grasses, and dwarf palmettos. But of all the plants of these curious tree-gardens the most striking and characteristic is the so-called Long Moss (Tillandsia usneoides). It drapes all the branches from top to bottom, hanging in long silvery-gray skeins, reaching a length of not less than eight or ten feet, and when slowly waving in the wind they produce a solemn funereal effect singularly impressive." (John Muir, *Camping in the Tombs*)

"For the dead and the living we must bear witness."–Elie Wiesel

𝄆𝄇

Holocaust Victim
Schmul Szcerkowski
Unknown-1945
Plot: Section O Lot 415

HERE LIETH
A THIRD OF THE ASHES OF 344
CREMATED SACRED SOULS,
VICTIMS OF THE NAZIS,
INCLUDING THE REMAINS OF
SCHMUL
SON OF Y'CHEEL SZCERKOWSKI
WHO WAS KILLED ON THE THIRD
OF NISON 5705-MAR.17,1945
BROUGHT HERE FROM ALEM,
HANOVER, GERMANY

Savannah is known for its religious diversity and Bonaventure Cemetery is no exception. Sections P Q S of Bonaventure was established in 1907 for the burial of Savannah's Jewish population if they so choose. There is a second entrance to Bonaventure to the right of the main gate. It has the Star of David at the entrance to recognize it as the entrance to the Jewish section.

One particular memorial has become a favorite to find and well worth seeking out if you have the chance to visit Bonaventure. It is the memorial of Schmul Szcerkowoski, a victim of the holocaust. If you face the Jewish chapel from the main road and look to the right of the stone arch you will see the memorial near the road. You will also see that many pebbles and small stones have been placed on top and around the memorial. It is a Jewish custom to use stones rather than flowers on the gravesites. Whatever the initial reason for placing a small stone on the memorials, it is seen as a symbolic gesture to honor the memory of the deceased person that is being visited.

Around 1950, Felix and his wife Manie Budek requested that the ashes of her father Schmul Szcerkowoski, a holocaust victim from the Nazi labor camp Alem in Hanover, Germany be sent to them here in The United States. They sent the ashes and the ashes of 343 other victims as well. How they determined that her father's ashes were truly part of what was sent is a mystery to me but the personal and intimate feeling of somehow having the ashes from there must have been overwhelming.

The memorial reads: "Here lieth a third of the ashes of 344 cremated souls, victims of the Nazis, including the remains of Schmul, son of Y'cheel Szcerkowoski, who was killed on the third of Nison 5705- Mar. 17, 1945 brought here from Alem, Hanover Germany"

**Entrance to the Jewish section
Of Bonaventure Cemetery**

**A menorah seen on many Jewish
Women's gravesites**

**Stones left in respect and remembrance of the
Deceased from visitors rather than flowers**

Looking in at the Jewish chapel in the cemetery.
This is the only chapel in the cemetery itself.

Symbol of the Cohen; represents members of the priestly tribe of
Aaron and is the greeting that would be given at the end of a
service. The lettering means "here lies"

The arch represents the entrance to Heaven and is
Found throughout Bonaventure.

Hidden away under some low branches in part of the Jewish section of Bonaventure, lies the remains of a young boy by the name of Edward Haynes Carter, who died at the age of 14.

His tombstone states that he was raised as a Bethesda Boy along with his brother George. Bethesda is one of the first orphanages in Georgia. For me, this is where the story became personal because my own father was raised by the state after the death of my grandmother and being abandoned by his father.

Edward is buried next to his mother, Dora Haynes Carter Wilkinson, who died in 1986 at the age of 80. Next to her is his sister Marrianne Mango, who was born one year after Edward. Marrianne died in 1984 at the age of 52. There is no mention if she was ever in a home. His brother George lies in a gravesite in front of his mother and siblings. I can't help but wonder what the circumstances were that Dora Hayes had to send her boys away. It must have been very hard on her. Whether or not he died while in their care has not been found out by myself as of yet, but a story that I would love to listen to.

Edward Haynes Carter

Dora Haynes

Noble and Wimberly Jones
1702-1775
Plot: Section D Lot: 13

Colonial Georgia

During the Civil War, families experienced the pain of division because of political views. Some family members were in support of the North and left their homes to fight with the Union armies; leaving families forever torn apart. This was true for the Revolutionary War as well. Families were divided between supporting King George II, the King of England and those wanting to live independently, making their own decisions about how to govern. Many of the parents of these families were raised in England and favored supporting their king. Their children, who had only known the colonies as their homeland, disagreed. This is how it was with the Jones Family of Savannah. To know more about Noble and Wimberly Jones, I should offer a little history on Colonial Georgia.

"Arriving late upon the stage of New World colonization, the British faced Spanish and French competition from the beginning. By 1732 the South Carolina colony marked the southern boundary of British America. Spanish to the South and French to the south and west posed constant threats to the wealth of Carolina. Raids by native allies and the threat of French and Spanish expansion supported the call for an additional colony. In 1732 King George II granted a charter to 21 Trustees to organize a new colony, Georgia. No slavery or alcohol was to be permitted." Noble Jones and his wife Sarah, their children Mary and son Noble Wimberly were part of this group that came with John Oglethorpe to

Georgia in 1733. "Jones requested and received the lease of 500 acres on the Isle of Hope, about ten miles south of Savannah. He dug a well and began construction of a fortified house he called "Wormsloe." Wormsloe was an ideal location to monitor traffic and scout for danger. In 1752 when Georgia became a Royal Colony, Jones received a Royal Grant for his Wormsloe holdings. He served on the Governor's Council, as Chief Justice, a Commander of the Miltia and Treasurer of the Colony. His loyalty to the King continued despite his son's ardent support of the Patriots as the Revolution neared. Noble Jones' death in 1775 saved his family from the open conflict marked by so many Georgia families when the revolution began in earnest. His death was probably the last of the original colonists who had arrived aboard the Anne some forty-two years before. With Jones death, his son, Noble Wimberly, assumed the family's leadership role in Georgia. Descendants of the original family still reside at this site and are actively involved in heritage preservation at Wormsloe." (Georgia Dept. of Natural Resources/Wormsloe State Historic Site)

There is an interesting story in regards to how the plantation got its name. When Noble Jones built the plantation he named it "Wormslow". Part of his plantation was dedicated to the production of silk so the name probably had to do with the silkworms that he used in his silk production. The name's spelling would be changed to Wormsloe a few generations down the line by one of Jones' decendents. It is the oldest plantation that still remains private to the descendants of Noble Jones.

Wimberly Jones married Sarah Davis in 1775 and they had fourteen children together. They outlived all their children except one.

This grave can be found towards the back of the cemetery and it almost sits in the road.
Surrounded by an iron fence it holds the remains of both Noble and Wimberly Jones.

John Mongin
1760-December 2, 1833
Plot: Section H lot 99.

John Mongin was the grandson of John David Mongin, who along with his brother Francis fled France because of religious persecution by the Catholic Church. The late 1600s was a time in world history where "Those who refused to embrace the church would be slaughtered or burned at the stakes. Word had spread that soldiers were nearing their village to persecute those Protestants and force them to convert.

The brothers collected what valuables and available money in their house, made their way by night to the sea shore where they hired a fishing boat to escape. They landed on the coast of England in 1725 and settled in England where they were watchmakers. Their own father did not make it out of France and was tortured so severely to make him renounce his religious beliefs that he died." Both brothers married and had children. Some of their children left England and migrated to South Carolina. John Mongin's father was one of those sons.

John Mongin was born in South May River in South Carolina on his family's plantation in 1760. A revolutionary soldier, he was married twice and had one child; an adopted daughter whom they named Mary Ann Naylor (now called Mary Ann Naylor Mongin).

John and his wife owned and worked a rice and cotton plantation on Daufuskie Island, South Carolina near his father. His wife died and was buried on the plantation. He remarried and left the plantation in the hand of overseers and moved to Savannah in 1797 where he became a merchant. He died in 1863 and was also buried at his plantation on Daufuskie Island. His obituary taken from The Daily Georgian dated December 2, 1833 reads:

"After a painful illness of fourteen days which he bore with the utmost patience and resignation, John David, one of the last revolutionary worthies. Age 71 year 11 months". (The Georgian Dec. 2, 1833)

His crypt was eventually relocated to Bonaventure Cemetery by floating it down the river on a large barge. It is said that his plot was chosen because of it close proximity to the river as it would have been very difficult to move it much further because of its weight. The crypt is in the shape of a pyramid and another example of the Egyptian revival style.

The Mongin crypt. It was moved by barge from Daufuskie Island, South Carolina to Bonaventure Cemetery. It is another example of Egyptian revival.

"There is, I am convinced, no picture that conveys in all its dreadfulness, a vision of sorrow, despairing, remediless, supreme. If I could paint such a picture, the canvas would show only a woman looking down at her empty arms." —Charolette Bronte

§§

Bonaventure's Children

What I find most heartbreaking about Bonaventure cemetery are the children. Savannah suffered several yellow fever outbreaks in the 1800's and my first thought was that they were lost to this fever. Records show however, that the yellow fever outbreaks took the lives of mainly young men; especially the Irish and German ethnic groups. During this time period the young men of these ethnic groups were mostly laborers working outside. They would often remove their shirts because of the heat and yellow fever was spread through mosquitos.

I am sure some children were lost through this fever and many others to childhood illness. Others were loss through accidents such as accidental drowning or in the case of Corrine Lawton, they took their own lives; older sons were lost in wars. I think about the day that they committed the tiny bodies to the grave, the tears that fell and about how often the parents would return to that place of burial, hoping somehow that it was all a bad dream. Something seems so wrong about a parent having to bury their child but Bonaventure holds evidence that many endured such pain and grief. Here are just a few that I came across on my wanderings through the cemetery.

"SOME SAY YOU ARE TOO PAINFUL TO
REMEMBER,
I SAY YOU ARE TOO BEAUTIFUL TO
FORGET"-unknown

∯

Mary and Emma Hartmann. Mary was born
June 5, 1858 died April 18th, 1869. (1.5 years old)
Her sister Emma was born Oct. 15th 1860 and died March 4,
1861
(5 months old)

Originally buried at Laurel Grove, the
Hartmann's were moved to Bonaventure.
They can be found in Section N near the road.

Children of C. & C. R. Hartmann

"Schwarz"
Four children from one family. Not one child lived
More than four years old.

Little Fred
Our only Son
"Safe with Jesus

Pearce and Catherine. Pearce was three when
He died and Catherine was two. Winged faces
Within clouds symbolize the children being carried
To Heaven.

Little Louisa Sindrat. Daughter of J.M. & S.A. Johnston
Born March 5, 1874 and died June 2, 1875 at the age
Of one year and three months. "Thy will be done."
The bird symbolizes God taking the child to rest
With him in Heaven.

Harry Green, youngest child of Benj; & Isabella Green
Died October 10, 1871 aged 8 years and 6 months
Epitaph reads "He shall gather lambs with his arm
And carry them in His bosom

Birds in general represent eternal life and the wreath represents
Eternal victory and eternity itself

Little Till aged 11 months and 24 days. Sleeping child
On a bed symbolizes a couple of things;
The bed represents at rest; sleep is the tie between
Life and death and the child represent innocence.
Pansies that are on the wreath signify remembrance and
humility.
I could not find a family name that was visible.

Willie lies to the left of Little Till.
I could not find a family name or any information
On his date of birth or death.

"Our babies"
Paulsen; one child died in 1871; the child other in 1873.
It does not give their age or parent's names.

In memory of my only little daughter
Catherine Johannah
Henriette Jahn
Born
Jan 21st 1872
Died Apl 9th 1875 years 3 months
Basler Family

Sacred to the memory of Joseph Chas
Son of W. and Mary M. Basler
Born 10th Sept. 1874
Died 15th Dec. 1879 aged 5 years 3 months and 1 day.
"Too young to die, too bright to live here now"

In memory of Maud Alena Basler
Born in Savannah Aug. 18th 1807
"Born but to die
Without a pity, with a sigh"

William M. Henry
Infant son of
Louis M & Phenie W. Warfield
The root from the live oak has through
The years, disrupted their son's gravesite

Sacred to the memory of Dora
Daughter of Fred & Dora Morgan
Born June 15th 1875
Died Sept. 8t 1880 aged 5 years 2 mos & 23 days
Dora has three symbols on her memorial; the weeping willow
represents mourning and grief; the lamb innocence and the
tombstone death; her family mourning over the death of their
innocent child.

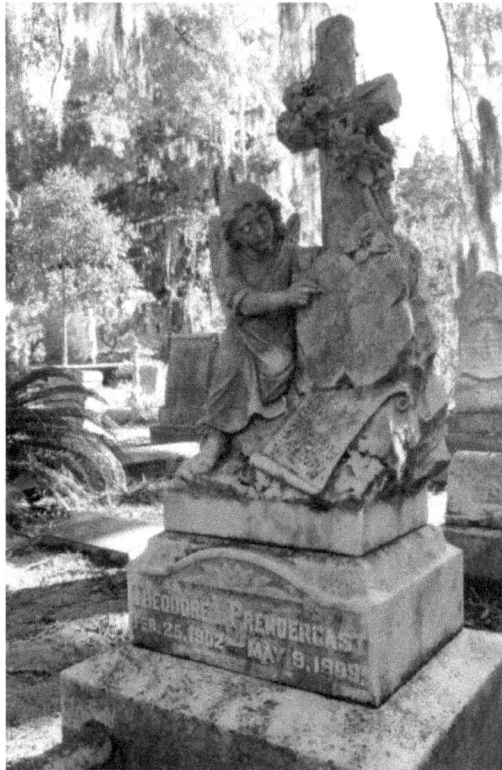

Theodore Prendercast
Feb. 25 1902- May 9, 1909
Theodore was seven when he died. The angel
Is writing on a stone heart "Papa's Sweetheart"
Below that on the scroll, it is written
"Our darling boy".   The careful detail
On this memorial clearly shows the grief
These parents felt at the loss of their little boy.

Lucy Bell Alexander was born Sept. 5th 1858
Died Nov. 22 1863 at the age of five years old.

**Alexander Children died within two days of each other
Can you imagine losing two children within a couple
of days of each other and the unbearable pain these
parents must have felt?**

William Alexander, Lucy's brother,
Born Jan 1, 1860 and died two days
Before his sister on Nov. 20th 1863
"He was all gentleness amiability and tenderness
Even when life promised most, how many hopes
Have withered"

Mary Catherine Roberts 1923-1926 age 3 years
Her parents are buried behind her
What I find intriguing is the small seal next to the
Rosebuds.
I found myself looking very close and it is indeed
a little seal that they had put into the design of her
Memorial.
It must have had some special meaning to her parents.

A small seal resting near a rose bud.
I have never encountered a small seal before.

Almost hidden from view by a palm tree
The only thing still legible was the date Aug. 1894

Albert A. M....(no longer legible)
Born Dec. 20, 1889
Died July 14, 1890
7months old

"All things must leave at one time or another. There is no perpetuity. No immortality; at least not on *this* earth."

– James Cracken

ꝕ

Etched In Stone

As you take your time exploring Bonaventure you will discover some very intimate thoughts that have been etched in stone. Some express the sorrow of loss, some the celebration of one's life and philosophies, while others express their faith in God and eternal hopes.

"When we at death must part
How keen How deep the pain
But we shall still be joined in Heart
And hope to meet again."

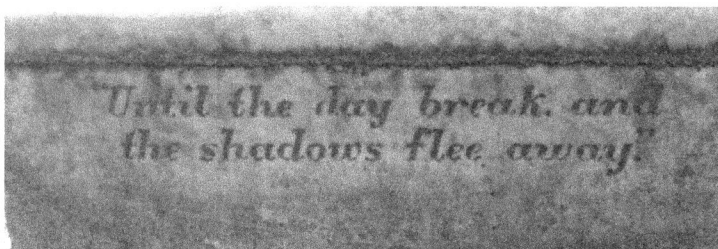

Until the day break and the shadows flee away

"We are the music makers,
We are the dreamers of dreams
We are the movers & Shakers
Of the world forever it seems."

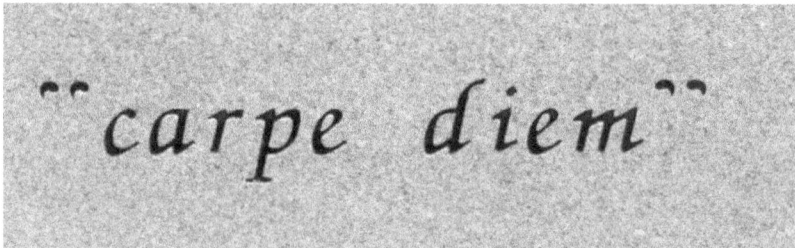

"Carpe diem"
Meaning seize the moment

"Adored Mother
Her boundless sense of
Curiosity about the world
Led to many happy adventures."
"I had a good run"

"There is no death! What seems so is transition;
This life of mortal breath
Is but a suburb of the life Elysian,
Whose portal we call death."

....Here are no storms,
No noise, but silence and eternal sleep."
Shakespeare

"Allured to brighter worlds and led the way."

"They shall be mine saith the Lord, in that day when
I make up my jewels"

"In the night of death hope sees
A Star
And listening love can hear
The rustle of a wing"

"Heaven's gentile stars united them in a love without end."

"Be of Good Courage"

"Behold I come quickly and my reward is with me
To give every man according as his works shall be
I am Alpha and Omega: The beginning and the End,
The first and the last"

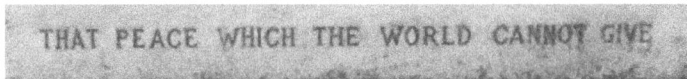

That Peace which the world cannot give

In an other and better world we shall desire more
Knowledge of thee.

"I am not afraid to die,
Having frequently thought of the issues
Of a dying hour

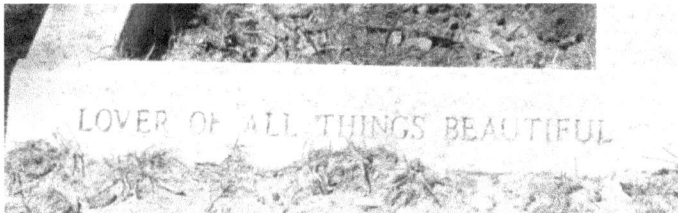

Lover of all things beautiful

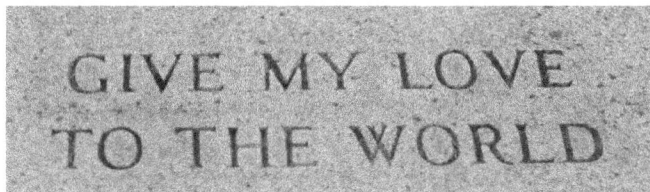

"Give my love to the world... inscribed on bench
In Conrad Aiken's plot."

"Does not the Savior hold her?
In his own arms and says of
Such is the Kingdom of Heaven
Farewell my precious child
My hope is to have thee
In full possession in a
Better place"

Born April 20, 1880. Died aboard the Battleship Illinois in
Cape Cod Bay. September 30, 1907 from injuries received
While on duty during a gale."

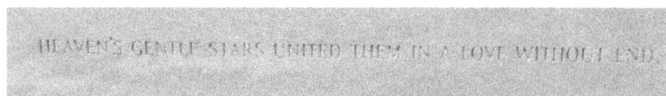

"Heaven's gentle stars united them in a love without end."

"His sweet mission ended
God has called him home"

"Did not live"

"Here lie side by side
Anthony Basler
And his beloved wife
Whom death could not divide"

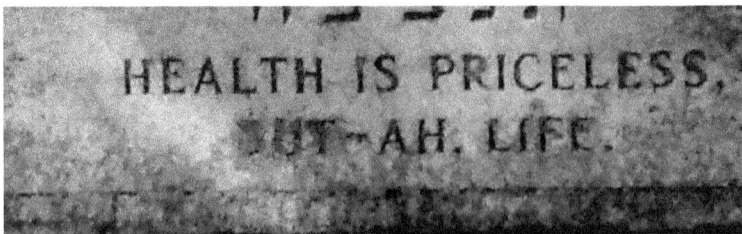

Health is priceless, but-ah life.

"Fair stranger whose feet have wondered to this land of silence. Contemplate this stone. Near it is interred dust which once a lovely form inhabited by a mind, superior in intelligence, warmth and amiableness to most of her sex. As a daughter, sister & friend; as a wife and mother for whom she left behind can boast so bright an example.

"Death lies on her like an untimely frost upon
The sweetest
Flower of all the field"

"Thy will be done"

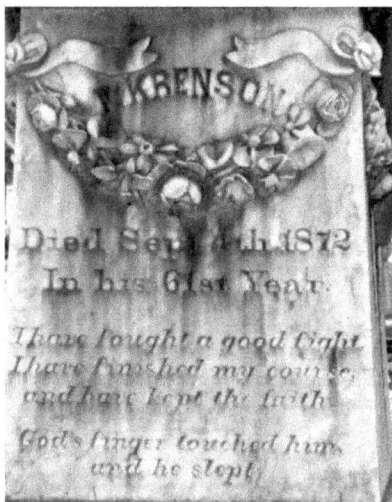

Krenson
Died Sept 4, 1872
In his 61st year
"I have fought a good fight
I have finished my course;
And have kept the faith.
God's finger touched him
And he slept."

Beauty within Her Walls

During the Victorian era symbols and motifs were used by the grieving family to express their devotion, thoughts, community standing, wealth and religious beliefs that they had about the afterlife. Bonaventure has so many that it would take many visits to see them all

Iron Works

Intricate iron fences surround many family plots

A fence post designed to look like

A burial urn draped with a mourning cloth

Details in Everything

What is left of an iron gate

A stone & iron fence surrounds this plot

From the smallest of gravestones to the highest of obelisks, Bonaventure is full of art worthy of any museum. Through photographs, I have tried to give you a glimpse of what this unique cemetery offers. Whether you walk the paths or drive through in your car, there is much to see. It is a place that certainly takes more than one visit to see all that it has to offer and even then there will be something that you missed and not realize it until the next time you find yourself following it paths. . You will find yourself saying how could I have missed this?

Crypts throughout Bonaventure

Many of the crypts have beautiful Stain glass within their walls

141

Two examples of the Egyptian revival that was Popular in the 1800's and early 1900's

William Gaston was a philanthropist and banker that lived in Savannah.

Gaston's tomb or the Strangers tomb was built in honor of William Gaston who was well known for his hospitality to those visiting Savannah. He would often lend his burial crypt to place visitors who died until their families could come and get their remains.

Originally located in Colonial Park Cemetery which is right in downtown historic Savannah. It was moved to Bonaventure and not surprisingly a stranger was still remaining in the tomb along with William Gaston. They remain enclosed together. I would imagine Mr. Gaston wouldn't mind.

Obelisks

Obelisk... Symbolic of the family's wealth and standing in the community. It also represents upward ascension to Heaven

In memory of our son, Robert S. Nicolson
Only son of John And Matilda Nicolson
Born at White bluff near Savannah GA
April 13, 1861
Drowned at Tybee Island,
July 10, 1881
20 years old

Symbols on this obelisk; oil lamp with full flame
Rose and burial cloth

The urn on top of the obelisk is
Symbolic of the souls
Ascension to heaven

Obelisks are not always tall. The cloth that
Covers the urn is symbolic of mourning
And usually is an
Indication that it was an older person

This one is so tall it towers above the trees

There are so many symbols on this short
Obelisk
The lion represent
The courage of the person as well as protection
From Evil. The wreath eternity burial
Cloth grief/death
His epitaph reads that he led a quiet but
Useful life and his death was regretted by
All who knew him

152

Crosses and Angels

There are so many angels and crosses within this cemetery that it would take a few days to really take the time to view the details on all of them. The symbolism, details and sometimes the size of each memorial that is displayed down every pathway can at times be overwhelming, especially when you stop to think that every memorial was placed here at the expense of the individual families. In the 1800's all this work was done by hand with a chisel and not with computerized equipment that automatically craves the design.

Keep this in mind if you ever get the chance to visit here or any other Victorian era cemetery and you perhaps will understand why people like me love to wander through these cities of the dead.

"So I will cherish the old rugged cross till my trophies at last I lay down and exchange it someday for a crown."– George Bennard

₷

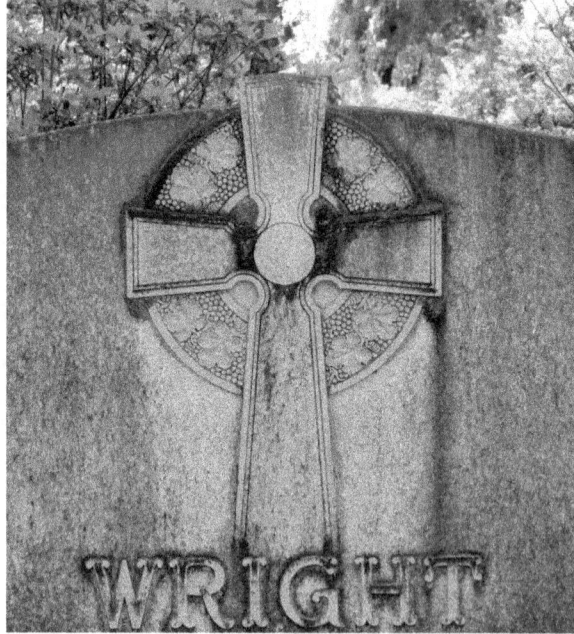

**The Celtic cross represents faith and eternity; ivy is symbolic
Of memory**

Copper cross embedded in stone

The rocks symbolize the foundation of the
Christian faith, the cross sits on that foundation which represents
Christ and the lilies represent the
Resurrection and eternal life.
Again this one all hand carved
William W. Rodgers
Died January 15, 1897
Aged 40 years
"Blessed are the pure in heart, for they shall see God

How wonderful to speak the language of angels, with no words for hate and a million words for love."-Freeman

ℱℱ

With finger pointing heavenward, this angel
Is holding something that has been broken
Through the years. If it is a sword, then this would
Be the Arch angel Michael that is showing the way
For the decease

The angel on this memorial has a pencil and book
Symbolizing that the deceased has been written
In the book of life or judgment.

**Outstretched arms on the angel symbolizes
Asking for God's mercy**

With the finger pointing upwards is an indication of the person's ascension to Heaven. This angel is holding a wreath which symbolizes eternity and victory

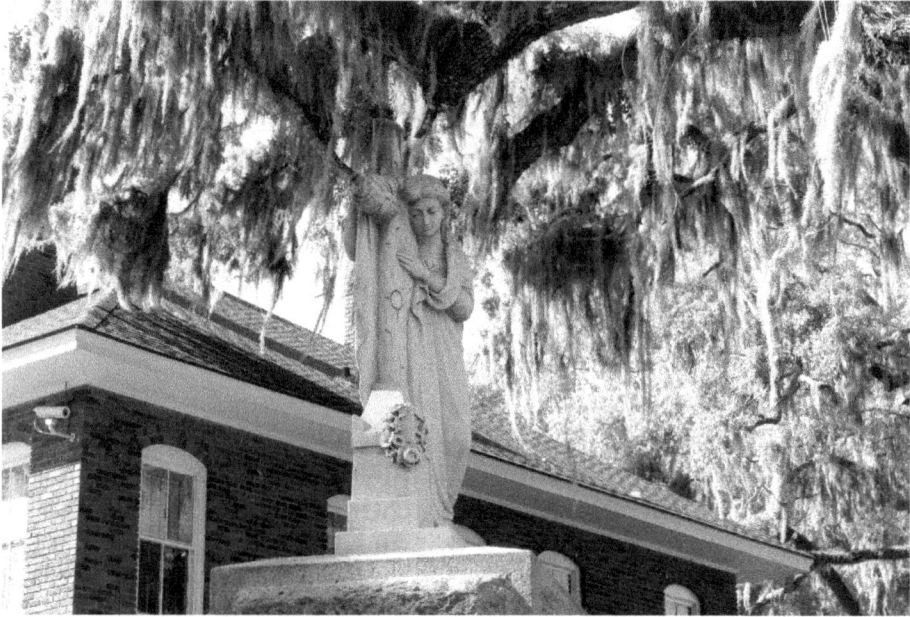

She greets the visitor as you drive through the entrance to
Bonaventure Cemetery. She leans on the cross as a symbol
Of clinging to her faith. The wreath is symbolic of eternity.

The weeping angel symbolizes grief

Angel holding crown and palm leaf which
Symbolizes the Victory, honor and resurrection of the just

Usually when a face is carved it is in the image
Of the deceased.

She is holding a wreath representing eternity and victory.
She seems to be thinking.

Another woman sitting with her hand in a
Thinking position. Perhaps an indication of her
Thoughts of eternal salvation. This one sits on rocks symbolizing
the Christian faith

A front view of the same statue. She is also
Holding a wreath which symbolizes eternity and victory.

"Far more powerful than religion, far more powerful than money, or even land or violence, are symbols. Symbols are stories. Symbols are pictures, or items, or ideas that represent something else. Human beings attach such meaning and importance to symbols that they can inspire hope, stand in for gods, or convince someone that he or she is dying. These symbols are everywhere around you." — Lia Habel

∯

Symbols

During the Victorian era symbols and motifs were used by the grieving family to express their devotion, thoughts, community standing, wealth and religious beliefs that they had about the afterlife. Bonaventure has so many that it would take many visits to see them all.

Columns represent a noble life and when the column is completed, it means a completed life.

Winged hourglass symbolizes how quickly life passes.
The burial cloth symbolizes death and mourning and
the fern friendship and remembrance... this one was
Carved by John Walz; a prominent sculptor from
Germany who called Savannah his home.

Crown symbolizes immortality, victory,
Honor and glory.
The cross represents a strong Christian faith.
"Be thou faithful unto death and I will give thee the Crown
Of life."(Rev. 2:10) It is the promised reward (the crown)
After the trials of life (cross)"

A copper wreath and sword which symbolizes a military
Service. Here he was a confederate soldier
Hamilton McDevit Branch
Born March 17, 1843
Died February 1899
Confederate Soldier

The oil lamp and the hand pouring oil into the lamp
Represent wisdom and faithfulness to the Lord.
The lamp has a bright flame symbolizing that it is full.
It sits on book representing the Bible, clouds would be the
Heaven. I love how the message is spoken through symbols.
What I am reading is that the deceased was faithful and obedient
to her faith and stayed prepared for her "groom"
(The Lord)

The clam has a couple of meanings.
It can represent
Rebirth it also represents the spiritual
Journey of the soul.
In Egyptian belief it represented the
Crossing over at the river.
When I saw this memorial I thought
Of the Biblical
Scripture of the Pearl of Great Price
And I certainly would relate that to my child.

A Bishop

The lily represents resurrection

There are soldiers from the civil war, both union
and confederate, the Spanish war, revolutionary war and
Every war since buried at Bonaventure...

The crossed sword usually symbolizes that the soldier loss
His life in battle

Confederate Soldier emblem

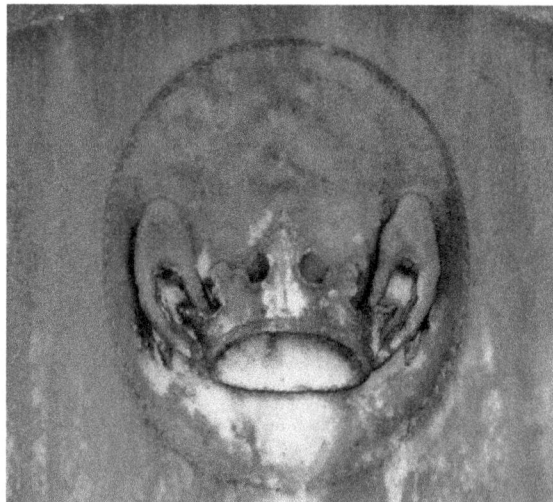

The crown symbolizes the reward of the just.
The crown of eternal life for the faithful in Christ.
The hands coming down from Heaven represents the hand of
God.

**Stars equal heaven, poppy symbolizes
Eternal sleep, cross, Christian faith**

**The hand reaching out for the rose bud is symbolic of God taking
The child to rest in Heaven with him and the rose bud represents
the age of the child**

"H" "I" "S" are the first 3 letters of Jesus' name in Greece...
"By this sign we conquer"

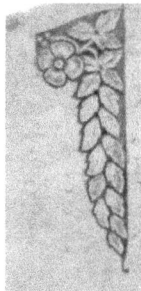

Pansy remembrance & humility

Knights of Pythiias   "Friendship, Charity, Benevolence

The roses not in full bloom usually are an indication
that the person was probably a young adult at death.

Clasped hands; seen on many married couples gravesites.
Usually the one who died first is the one taking the other hand
to show the way to heaven. The cuffs on the woman will usually
have frills. Holding onto the cross represents clinging to the
cross
and faith.

Not sure what this one stands for. The words Sovereignty
are still visible;

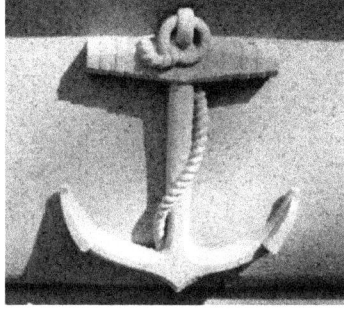

The anchor meant stability in faith, also an occupational
Symbol representing a naval or seaman. The broken rope
Or chain is the cessation of life

The hand reaching down from the clouds symbolizes
God reaching from Heaven
To take the decease to Heaven... The rose bud shows
that it was someone young

"The winged globe is a symbol out of the Egyptian revival that was popular in the 1800's and early 1900's it symbolizes the Soul without physical form; also a symbol of divine power three rows of feathers represent good words, good thoughts and good deeds.

Torch ablaze means immortality
An inverted torch is death and a life extinguished

**Straight edge ruler and hammer.
The deceased was most probable a
Carpenter by profession**

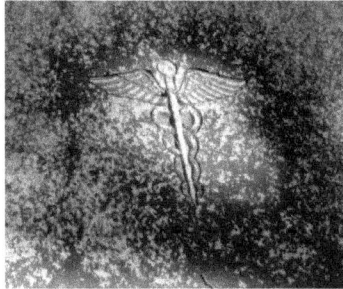

Medical profession; doctor

The thistle is a symbol of grief and mourning

Sheaves of wheat represent a fruitful life; usually
Found on older person's gravesites.

Star of David symbolizes divine protection

**The hand of God reaching down for the deceased
Proclaiming the written word "Blessed are the pure
In heart for they shall see God."**

**The acorn is symbolic of potential; with leaves maturity
And old age.**

Columns; a life complete with the urn symbolic of the soul

Slave Tiles

"Slave tiles" Four plantations made these from wooden molds. This folk art is very much a part of Bonaventure

**I found four separate designs and wonder
if each plantation had its own**

**More slave tiles; some have been broken
through the years**

"Everything has beauty, but not everyone sees it."-Confuicus

ﬀﬆ

**Erosion over time as almost destroyed this carving
of a young girl sleeping**

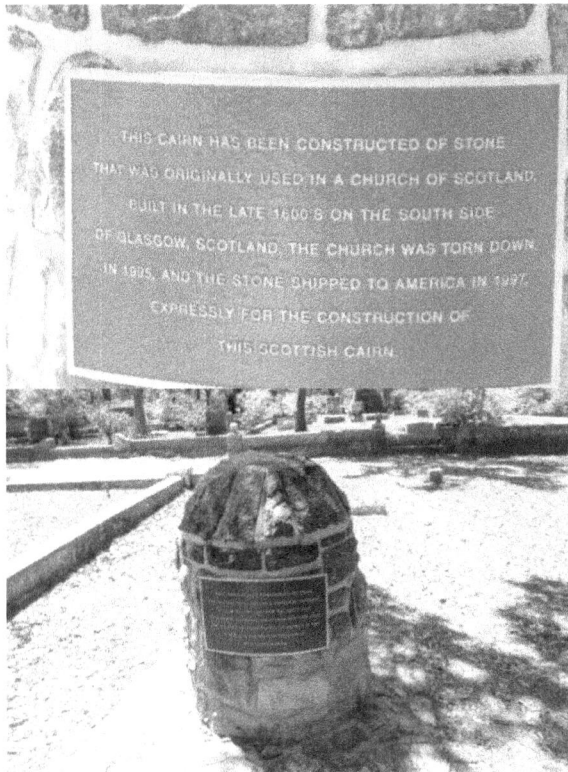

Cairn constructed of stone that was originally used
in a Church of Scotland. Built in the late 1600's on the
South Side of Glasgow, Scotland. The Church was torn
down in 1995 and the stone shipped to America in 1997
Expressly for the construction of this Scottish Cairn.

196

Table top memorial; seen especially in the
1700's

A leg to another table that wasn't there unless the tops were just
Placed on the ground; I do not know how this one fell over.
It would be sad to think that
Someone did this on purpose. Where the other legs have moved
Is still another unanswered question.

Another memorial stone that has been knocked over.
Time has also eroded most of the
Inscription what remains;
Catherine Gould
Daughter of
Not legible
Born 1875
Died January 12th 1875
The lily represents a resurrected life and the resurrection

Almost hidden from view, a former Savannah police officer. He lies in the Jewish section of Bonaventure.

Gothic Greek Orthodox style

203

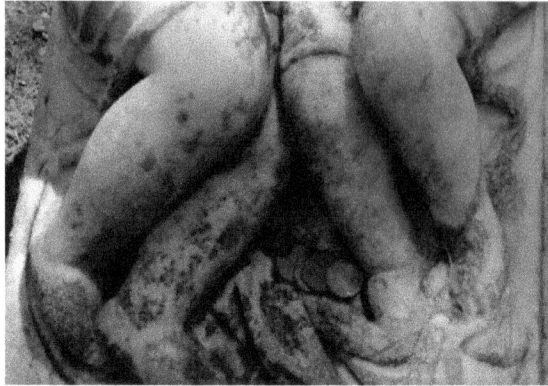

I have seen several memorials where visitors have
Left coins, especially at children's gravesites.
This actually damages the stone
If a visitor wants to leave coins they should place
them nearby on the ground to prevent any damage to
The memorial itself.

Columns torch with blazing flame and the
Arch I like
the angle of the photo to show the cross within
the gate
To Heaven.

I love this woman's smile. She is placed in
The newer section of Bonaventure.
Bonaventure is an active cemetery that still
Sells plots at this time. On my last visit, several
Burials were taking place in the older section

"Death is not a foe, but an inevitable adventure."–Sir Oliver Lodge

ﬀ

Other Notables

Faces of Bonaventure

Intermingled between the oak trees and grandeur of this old Victorian-era cemetery are burial plots with names many would be familiar with. There is Revolutionary and Civil War Officers who are written in the history books because of their accomplishments and sacrifices made to the country and state. Many founding fathers of Savannah are buried here as well. There are silent screen actors, composers, songwriters, and a Pulitzer Prize winning poet. All those accomplishments are just part of the past and they have closed their eyes to this mortal existence. Swords and guns have been laid down and the distance wars have been put away in history books. The writer's thoughts and the film stars are confined to books and old films that are seldom seen. If you take a minute or two to think about all the faces that are buried here in Bonaventure and realize that each of these people has unique gifts that were theirs alone, it can be quite sad to realize that those gifts were laid to rest as well. "As the stately ships go to their haven over the hill, but oh for the touch of a vanished hand and the sound of a voice that is still.

Edythe Chapman was considered "Hollywood's mother. She was born in New York in 1863. She was a stage actress. She married James Neil, from Savannah, GA after meeting him in Cincinnati, Ohio while working in his stock company. They were married in 1897 and made movies together with Cecil

B Demile where they had roles in his movie the Ten Commandments. She also played Aunt Polly in Huckleberry Finn. She died in Glendale CA in 1948 and interred at Bonaventure. She was eighty-five when she died. Her husband died in March 1931. Thy both are buried in Bonaventure Cemetery. (No photo available)

Conrad Aiken was born in Savannah August 5 1889. Aiken was orphaned at the age of eleven when his father killed his mother and then himself. Distant relatives raised in him in Massachusetts. He studied at Harvard where one of his classmates was TS Elliot. Aiken won the Pulitzer for his "Selected Poems". He was the publishing agent for Emily Dickens and was given much credit for her success. He often visited his own parent's gravesites and wanted to extend that to others who should visit him. It has been said that he wanted his tombstone to be a bench so that poetry lovers could sit there and enjoy a drink or two. He died in Savannah August 17 1973 at the age of eighty- four.

**Conrad Aiken's wife was an artist
In her own right.**

Aiken's epitaph

..Songwriter of over 1,000 songs including Moon River. He, his wife and mother are buried in Bonaventure next to him. It was rumored that he had an affair with the late Judy Garland

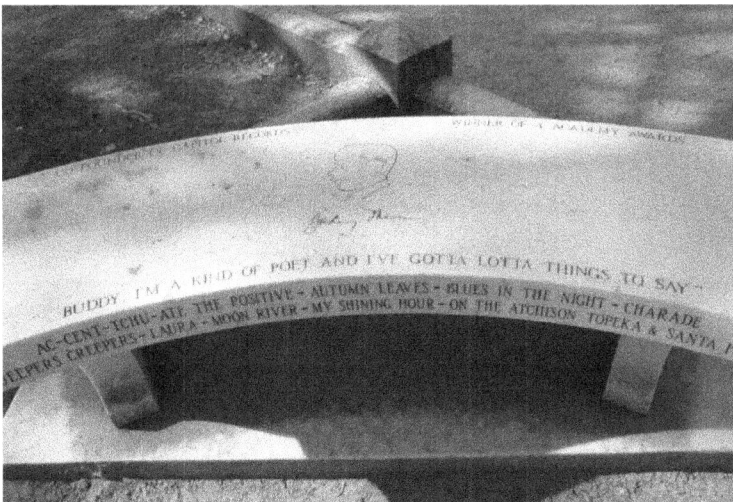

A bench that Johnny wanted place in his plot so that people could sit and visit awhile; perhaps enjoy a glass of wine as he would do when he often
Visited his mother after she died in 1977.

His mother's gravesite

**Johnny Mercer's Mother's memorial and gravesite
"My mama done told me"**

Johnny Mercer's wife Ginger
"You must have been a beautiful baby"

Johnny Mercer.
"And the angels sing"

The river that inspired the famous song "Moon River"

"Moon River, wider than a mile,
I'm crossing you in style someday.
Oh, dream maker, you heart breaker;
wherever you're going I'm going your way.
Two drifters off to see the world.
There's such a lot of world to see.
We're after the same rainbow's end--
waiting 'round the bend,
my huckleberry friend,
Moon River and me."-Johnny Mercer

♬

Epilogue

"Of death among our own species, to say nothing of the thousand styles and modes of murder, our best memories, even among happy deaths, yield groans and tears, mingled with morbid exultation; burial companies, black in cloth and countenance; and, last of all, a black box burial in an ill-omened place, haunted by imaginary glooms and ghosts of every degree. Thus death becomes fearful, and the most notable and incredible thing heard around a death-bed is, "I fear not to die."

But let children walk with Nature, let them see the beautiful blending and communions of death and life, their joyous inseparable unity, as taught in woods and meadows, plains and mountains and streams of our blessed star, and they will learn that death is stingless indeed, and as beautiful as life, and that the grave has no victory, for it never fights. All is divine harmony." (John Muir)

My grandson deep within Bonaventure
It was not a fearful place for him but rather an
Adventure of epic proportion.

Noticing a family
Of four children

Children should be taught that cemeteries are
Not places to fear, but rather that they are rich in history.

"Life is much shorter than I imagined it to be."
-Abraham Cahan

ʄʄ

My Grandsons walking the pathways

It was my granddaughter who found Edward for me... It was as if we had found a family member and we all celebrated when we found his location

My family walking down one of the many roads
And paths within the cemetery.

My daughters and their sons. Bonaventure was to them a serene
and tranquil Place to wander through.

My daughter and grandsons placing stones
On the memorial for the holocaust victims as a token
Of respect. A wonderful learning opportunity
of past History. A lesson that surpasses what they
would have learned in the classroom.

On this particular day we were at Bonaventure over three hours.
I know that they were tired at times,
but not once did any of the grandkids asked to leave
or when we would be leaving.

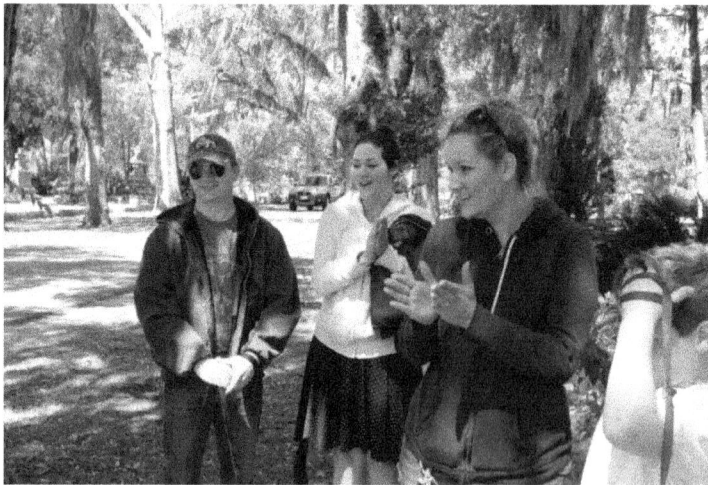

My youngest grandson started singing to one of the gravesites;
We were of course we impressed.

Pondering life

My daughter became somewhat emotional over this
Grave of a Jewish woman who happened to have
The same name as me.

My son and grandson looking for stain glass art in the crypt

**My sister who has made a couple of trips
With me to Bonaventure and other cemeteries
Located in the Southern regions**

Even the dogs took in Bonaventure

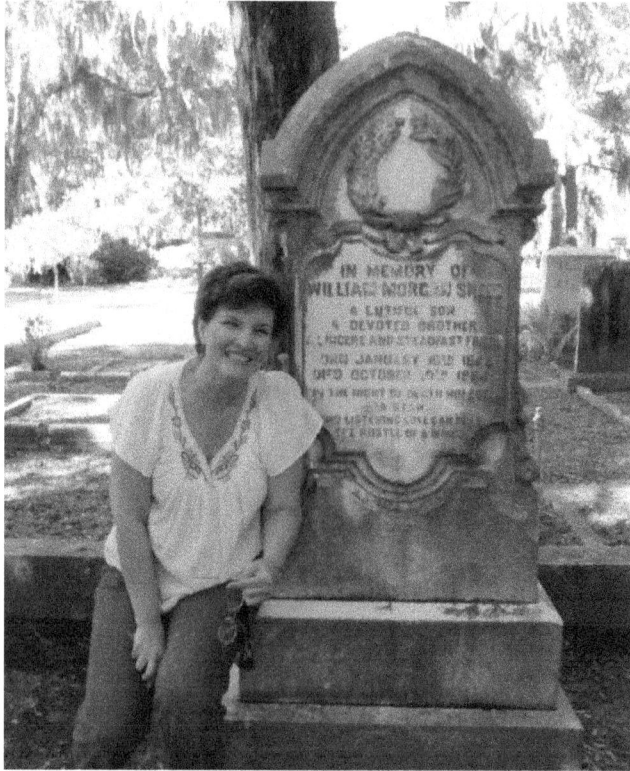

The author enjoying herself very much

"The privilege of a lifetime is being who you are."

-Joseph Campbell

∯

"In Three Words I can sum up everything I've

learned about life: It goes on."-Robert Frost

ﬀﬆ

Bonaventure cemetery is opened free to the public daily

Pets must be kept on a leash

8 am – 5pm.

References

1.   The Southern Historic Collection collection number: 00415 collection title: Alexander Robert Lawton Papers, 1774-1952 The Wilson Library, And University of North Carolina at Chapel Hill. Alexander J. Lawton obituary, Savannah Morning news, 1877-edition   Jan.   1-Dec   31,   1877,   pg. 337http://.lib.unc.edu/mss/inv/1/Lawton, Alexander_Robert.html
http://ruthrawls.worpress.com/2010/07/18/corrinne-elliot-lawton

2.   Wakelyn, Jon (2012, June 4). "Biographical dictionary of the Confederacy." Page, 278; "Dictionary of American Biography."; Volume 11; page 61.

3.   Muir, John "A Thousand Mile Walk to the Gulf." Chapter IV "Camping among the Tombs." Pages 69, 70, 71.

4.   "The Live Oak Trees of Bonaventure."   "Bonaventure Plantation.";   "Bonaventure   History." http://www.savannahga.gov/cityweb/cemeteriesweb.nsf/

5.   Watson, Wales, J. Http://trees.ancestry.com/treewaston; city directory 1900 6.   Hervey passenger list; city directory Http:// trees.ancestry.com/tree city directory 1925, us passport application

7.   c-spanvideo.org/program/300167; interview with Dorothy W. Kingery; C-span2booktv.org

8.   "The Savannah Chronicles: The killing of Danny Hansford by Jim   Williams." http:www.channelingricky.com/2012/11/savannah

9.   gastateparks.org/wormsloe

10.   Bonaventure Historical Society

11.   http://findagrave.com Jims Williams, Noble Jones, wimberly jones, harry Hervey

12.   http://ancestry.com Frances and wales Watson burial index

13. Georgia Historical Society personal letters text Harry Hervey/Carleton Hildreth

14.   Savannah Now http://www. Georgia History.com

15.   vintageviews.org/vv-tl/pages/cem_symbolism.htm; "Glossary of Victorian Cemetery Symbolism-Vintage Views."

16.   http://www.lib.niu.ed/2003/ih110603.html "Graven images-Illinois periodicals

17.   Marshall, Mary-will-record Book 4Q Chatham County, Georgia, Superior court folios 88-91 photo stated copy GHS

18.   Savannah Daily Morning News 1850-56, 1860-62. Savannah News & Harold 1806, 1867

19.   1890 Georgia property tax digest.

20.   Taliaferro/Marshall, Index to wills 1796-1817, 1845, 1866, 1892, 1893, and 1928

21.   Death Notice of Mary Leaver Marshall, March 6, 7, 8, 1976. Savannah Morning News 29 Jan 1877, May 10, 1877.

22.   Savannah Female Asylum Minute Book 1839, pg. 410

23.   Georgia Historical Society Marshall files 20

24.   Christ Church of Savannah Baptism Book; Georgia Historical Society.

25.   Marshall-Barclay divorce proceedings, judgment book C #9402, Chatham County, Georgia Superior court (copy Marshall file-GA Historical Society.

26.   Marshall, 1840 adoption document GHS

27.   1880 census enumeration district 023 Image 0412 Charles Taliaferro

28.   Savannah GA Roll 138 film 1254128, 1882, 1883-1886, 1888, 1890 Savannah city directories Charles Taliaferro

29.   Wales/Frances Watson; 1910 Census C.T. Madison Orange county, VA Roll T624 1640 page 7B end 0089, image 169, FHL microfilm 137563

30.   US city directories Savannah, GA 1821-1989 1888, 1891, 1897, 1901, 1904

31.   1880 Census, Bradford, Orange, Vermont, Albany Cemetery Association 1791-2011 Menand, NY, Albany Rural Cemetery burial Cards

32.   Gilmore/Walz; US city directories 1915; passport application 1895-1905, 1874-1882 roll 2/9-01 Sept. 1877-30 Nov 1877.

33 Http://.www.sip.armstrong.edu/warlick/marshall.rtf

34. Http://www.gastateparks.org/wormsloe

35.   Holcomb, Brent H. South Carolina Marriages. 1688-1799 Baltimore; Genealogy Publishing Company Inc. 1980

36.   Harden William, A History of Savannah and South Georgia. Vol 1 Chicago and New York. The Lewis publishing Company, 1913

37.   Heitman, F.B.   Historical Pegister of Officers of the Continental Army during the War of the Revolution, 1973

www.ingramcontent.com/pod-product-compliance
Lightning Source LLC
Chambersburg PA
CBHW081510040426
42447CB00013B/3177